To:

_____

From:

_____

Poems for Morning

STERLING
New York

STERLING
New York

An Imprint of Sterling Publishing Co., Inc.

STERLING and the distinctive Sterling logo are registered trademarks
of Sterling Publishing Co., Inc.

Cover illustration and compilation © 2022 Sterling Publishing Co., Inc.

ISBN 978-1-4549-4477-5

Library of Congress Control Number: 2021951605

Distributed in Canada by Sterling Publishing Co., Inc.
c/o Canadian Manda Group, 664 Annette Street
Toronto, Ontario M6S 2C8, Canada
Distributed in the United Kingdom by GMC Distribution Services
Castle Place, 166 High Street, Lewes, East Sussex BN7 1XU, England
Distributed in Australia by NewSouth Books
University of New South Wales, Sydney, NSW 2052, Australia

For information about custom editions, special sales, and premium and
corporate purchases, please contact Sterling Special Sales at
specialsales@sterlingpublishing.com.

Manufactured in the United States

2 4 6 8 10 9 7 5 3

sterlingpublishing.com

Interior design by Rich Hazelton

Contents

Dawn

Morning

The Day Ahead

Dawn

To Morning

William Blake

O holy virgin! clad in purest white,
Unlock heav'n's golden gates, and issue forth;
Awake the dawn that sleeps in heaven; let light
Rise from the chambers of the east, and bring
The honey'd dew that cometh on waking day.
O radiant morning, salute the sun,
Round like a huntsman to the chase, and with
Thy buskin'd feet appear upon our hills.

The Promise of the Morning Star

Amy Lowell

Thou father of the children of my brain
    By thee engendered in my willing heart,
    How can I thank thee for this gift of art
Poured out so lavishly, and not in vain.

What thou created never more can die,
    Thy fructifying power lives in me
    And I conceive, knowing it is by thee,
Dear other parent of my poetry!

For I was but a shadow with a name,
    Perhaps by now the very name's forgot;
    So strange is Fate that it has been my lot
To learn through thee the presence of that aim

Which evermore must guide me. All unknown,
    By me unguessed, by thee not even dreamed,
    A tree has blossomed in a night that seemed
Of stubborn, barren wood. For thou hast sown

This seed of beauty in a ground of truth.
    Humbly I dedicate myself, and yet
    I tremble with a sudden fear to set
New music ringing through my fading youth.

Hymn Before Sun-Rise, in the Vale of Chamouni

Samuel Taylor Coleridge

Hast thou a charm to stay the morning-star
In his steep course? So long he seems to pause
On thy bald awful head, O sovran BLANC,
The Arve and Arveiron at thy base
Rave ceaselessly; but thou, most awful Form!
Risest from forth thy silent sea of pines,
How silently! Around thee and above
Deep is the air and dark, substantial, black,
An ebon mass: methinks thou piercest it,
As with a wedge! But when I look again,
It is thine own calm home, thy crystal shrine,
Thy habitation from eternity!
O dread and silent Mount! I gazed upon thee,
Till thou, still present to the bodily sense,
Didst vanish from my thought: entranced in prayer
I worshipped the Invisible alone.

Yet, like some sweet beguiling melody,
So sweet, we know not we are listening to it,
Thou, the meanwhile, wast blending with my Thought,
Yea, with my Life and Life's own secret joy:
Till the dilating Soul, enrapt, transfused,
Into the mighty vision passing—there
As in her natural form, swelled vast to Heaven!

Awake, my soul! not only passive praise
Thou owest! not alone these swelling tears,
Mute thanks and secret ecstasy! Awake,
Voice of sweet song! Awake, my heart, awake!
Green vales and icy cliffs, all join my Hymn.

Thou first and chief, sole sovereign of the Vale!
O struggling with the darkness all the night,
And visited all night by troops of stars,
Or when they climb the sky or when they sink:
Companion of the morning-star at dawn,
Thyself Earth's rosy star, and of the dawn
Co-herald: wake, O wake, and utter praise!
Who sank thy sunless pillars deep in Earth?
Who filled thy countenance with rosy light?
Who made thee parent of perpetual streams?

And you, ye five wild torrents fiercely glad!
Who called you forth from night and utter death,
From dark and icy caverns called you forth,
Down those precipitous, black, jagged rocks,
For ever shattered and the same for ever?
Who gave you your invulnerable life,
Your strength, your speed, your fury, and your joy,
Unceasing thunder and eternal foam?
And who commanded (and the silence came),
Have let the billows stiffen, and have rest?

Ye Ice-falls! ye that from the mountain's brow
Adown enormous ravines slope amain—
Torrents, methinks, that heard a mighty voice,

And stopped at once amid their maddest plunge!
Motionless torrents! silent cataracts!
Who made you glorious as the Gates of Heaven
Beneath the keen full moon? Who bade the sun
Clothe you with rainbows? Who, with living flowers
Of loveliest blue, spread garlands at your feet?—
GOD! let the torrents, like a shout of nations,
Answer! and let the ice-plains echo, GOD!
GOD! sing ye meadow-streams with gladsome voice!
Ye pine-groves, with your soft and soul-like sounds!
And they too have a voice, yon piles of snow,
And in their perilous fall shall thunder, GOD!

Ye living flowers that skirt the eternal frost!
Ye wild goats sporting round the eagle's nest!
Ye eagles, play-mates of the mountain storm!
Ye lightnings, the dread arrows of the clouds!
Ye signs and wonders of the element!
Utter forth God, and fill the hills with praise!

Thou too, hoar Mount! With thy sky-pointing peaks,
Oft from whose feet the avalanche, unheard,
Shoots downward, glittering through the pure serene
Into the depths of clouds, that veil thy breast—
Thou too again, stupendous Mountain! Thou
That as I raise my head, awhile bowed low
In adoration, upward from thy base
Slow traveling with dim eyes suffused with tears,
Solemnly seemest, like a vapor cloud,
To rise before me—Rise, O ever rise,
Rise like a cloud of incense from the Earth!

Thou kingly Spirit throned among the hills,
Thou dread ambassador from Earth to Heaven,
Great Hierarch! tell thou the silent sky,
And tell the stars, and tell yon rising sun
Earth, with her thousand voices, praises GOD.

Moon in the Morning

Mary Eleanor Roberts

What dost thou, so ghostly white
    In the halls of day?—
Facing the triumphant light,
    Revelers astray?

When thy silver court was kept,
    Thou and thine were free,
And the sun, while dotards slept,
    Did not spy on thee.

Scent of jasmine, voices low,
    Dost thou seek them yet—
Lovers of the long ago
    Thou canst not forget?

Day's gay banners all unfurled
    Flaunt from sea to sea:
All the work of all the world
    Calls the sun and me.

Nay, thou shall not bid me stand!
    Nay, I will not yield!
Strong to-day in my right hand
    Is the brand I wield.

Then anoint thee, shadows fly!
　　Wherefore haunt me so—
Hanging mournful in the sky,
　　Pale and loath to go?

Sunrise on the Hills

Henry Wadsworth Longfellow

I stood upon the hills, when heaven's wide arch
Was glorious with the sun's returning march,
And woods were brightened, and soft gales
Went forth to kiss the sun-clad vales.
The clouds were far beneath me;—bathed in light,
They gathered mid-way round the wooded height,
And, in their fading glory, shone
Like hosts in battle overthrown.
As many a pinnacle, with shifting glance.
Through the gray mist thrust up its shattered lance,
And rocking on the cliff was left
The dark pine blasted, bare, and cleft.
The veil of cloud was lifted, and below
Glowed the rich valley, and the river's flow
Was darkened by the forest's shade,
Or glistened in the white cascade;
Where upward, in the mellow blush of day,
The noisy bittern wheeled his spiral way.

I heard the distant waters dash,
I saw the current whirl and flash,—
And richly, by the blue lake's silver beach,
The woods were bending with a silent reach,
Then o'er the vale, with gentle swell,
The music of the village bell
Came sweetly to the echo-giving hills;

And the wild horn, whose voice the woodland fills,
Was ringing to the merry shout,
That faint and far the glen sent out,
Where, answering to the sudden shot, thin smoke,
Through thick-leaved branches, from the dingle broke.

    If thou art worn and hard beset
With sorrows, that thou wouldst forget,
If thou wouldst read a lesson, that will keep
Thy heart from fainting and thy soul from sleep,
Go to the woods and hills!—No tears
Dim the sweet look that Nature wears.

Spring Morning

A. E. Housman

Star and coronal and bell
    April underfoot renews,
And the hope of man as well
    Flowers among the morning dews.

Now the old come out to look,
    Winter past and winter's pains,
How the sky in pool and brook
    Glitters on the grassy plains.

Easily the gentle air
    Wafts the turning season on;
Things to comfort them are there,
    Though 'tis true the best are gone.

Now the scorned unlucky lad
    Rousing from his pillow gnawn
Mans his heart and deep and glad
    Drinks the valiant air of dawn.

Half the night he longed to die,
    Now are sown on hill and plain
Pleasures worth his while to try
    Ere he longs to die again.

Blue the sky from east to west
    Arches, and the world is wide,
Though the girl he loves the best
    Rouses from another's side.

The Cloud

Percy Bysshe Shelley

I bring fresh showers for the thirsting flowers,
    From the seas and the streams;
I bear light shade for the leaves when laid
    In their noonday dreams.
From my wings are shaken the dews that waken
    The sweet buds every one,
When rocked to rest on their mother's breast,
    As she dances about the sun.
I wield the flail of the lashing hail,
    And whiten the green plains under,
And then again I dissolve it in rain,
    And laugh as I pass in thunder.

I sift the snow on the mountains below,
    And their great pines groan aghast;
And all the night 'tis my pillow white,
    While I sleep in the arms of the blast.
Sublime on the towers of my skiey bowers,
    Lightning my pilot sits,
In a cavern under is fettered the thunder,
    It struggles and howls at fits;
Over earth and ocean, with gentle motion
    This pilot is guiding me,
Lured by the love of the genii that move
    In the depths of the purple sea;
Over the rills, and the crags, and the hills,

Over the lakes and the plains,
Wherever he dream, under mountain or stream,
    The Spirit he loves remains;
And I all the while bask in Heaven's blue smile,
    Whilst he is dissolving in rains.

The sanguine Sunrise, with his meteor eyes,
    And his burning plumes outspread,
Leaps on the back of my sailing rack,
    When the morning star shines dead.
As on the jag of a mountain crag,
    Which an earthquake rocks and swings,
An eagle alit one moment may sit
    In the light of its golden wings.
And when Sunset may breathe, from the lit sea beneath,
    Its ardours of rest and of love,
And the crimson pall of eve may fall
    From the depth of Heaven above,
With wings folded I rest, on mine airy nest,
    As still as a brooding dove.

That orbed maiden with white fire laden,
    Whom mortals call the moon,
Glides glimmering o'er my fleece-like floor,
    By the midnight breezes strewn;
And wherever the beat of her unseen feet,
    Which only the angels hear,
May have broken the woof of my tent's thin roof,
    The stars peep behind her and peer;
And I laugh to see them whirl and flee,
    Like a swarm of golden bees,
When I widen the rent in my wind-built tent,

Till calm the rivers, lakes, and seas,
Like strips of the sky fallen through me on high,
Are each paved with the moon and these.

I bind the sun's throne with a burning zone,
And the Moon's with a girdle of pearl;
The volcanoes are dim, and the stars reel and swim,
When the whirlwinds my banner unfurl.
From cape to cape, with a bridge-like shape,
Over a torrent sea,
Sunbeam-proof, I hang like a roof,
The mountains its columns be.
The triumphal arch through which I march
With hurricane, fire, and snow,
When the powers of the air are chained to my chair,
Is the million-coloured bow;
The sphere-fire above its soft colours wove,
While the moist Earth was laughing below.

I am the daughter of earth and water,
And the nursling of the sky:
I pass through the pores of the ocean and shores;
I change, but I cannot die.
For after the rain when with never a stain
The pavilion of heaven is bare,
And the winds and sunbeams with their convex gleams,
Build up the blue dome of air,
I silently laugh at my own cenotaph,
And out of the caverns of rain,
Like a child from the womb, like a ghost from the tomb,
I arise and unbuild it again.

Dawn

❧

William Butler Yeats

I would be ignorant as the dawn
That has looked down
On that old queen measuring a town
With the pin of a brooch,
Or on the withered men that saw
From their pedantic Babylon
The careless planets in their courses,
The stars fade out where the moon comes.
And took their tablets and did sums;
I would be ignorant as the dawn
That merely stood, rocking the glittering coach
Above the cloudy shoulders of the horses;
I would be—for no knowledge is worth a straw—
Ignorant and wanton as the dawn.

The Dawn Wind

Rudyard Kipling

At two o'clock in the morning, if you open your window
and listen,
You will hear the feet of the Wind that is going to call
the sun.
And the trees in the shadow rustle, and the trees in the
moonlight glisten,
And though it is deep, dark night, you feel that the night
is done.

So do the cows in the field. They graze for an hour and
lie down,
Dozing and chewing the cud; or a bird in the ivy wakes,
Chirrups one note and is still, and the restless Wind
stares on,
Fidgeting far down the road, till, softly, the darkness
breaks.

Back comes the Wind full strength with a blow like an
angel's wing,
Gentle but waking the world, as he shouts: "The Sun!
The Sun!"
And the light floods over the fields and the birds begin
to sing,
And the Wind dies down in the grass. It is Day and his
work is done.

So when the world is asleep, and there seems no hope
 of her waking
Out of some long, bad dream that makes her mutter
 and moan,
Suddenly, all men arise to the noise of fetters breaking,
And every one smiles at his neighbour and tells him
 his soul is his own!

Morning-Watch

Henry Vaughan

O joyes! infinite sweetness! with what flowres
And shoots of glory my soul breakes and buds!
    All the long hours
    Of night, and rest,
    Through the still shrouds
    Of sleep, and clouds,
  This dew fell on my breast;
    Oh, how it bloods
And spirits all my earth! heark! in what rings
And hymning circulations the quick world
    Awakes and sings;
    The rising winds
    And falling springs,
    Birds, beasts, all things
  Adore him in their kinds.
    Thus all is hurl'd
In sacred hymnes and order, the great chime
And symphony of nature. Prayer is
    The world in tune,
    A spirit-voyce,
    And vocall joyes,
  Whose Eccho is heaven's blisse.
    O let me climb
When I lye down! The pious soul by night

Is like a clouded star whose beams, though said
        To shed their light
        Under some cloud,
        Yet are above,
        And shine and move
     Beyond that misty shrowd.
        So in my bed,
That curtain'd grave, though sleep, like ashes, hide
My lamp and life, both shall in thee abide.

When I heard at the close of the day

Walt Whitman

When I heard at the close of the day how my name
      had been receiv'd with plaudits in the capitol,
      still it was not a happy night for me that follow'd,
And else when I carous'd, or when my plans were
      accomplish'd, still I was not happy,
But the day when I rose at dawn from the bed of perfect
      health, refresh'd, singing, inhaling the ripe breath
      of autumn,
When I saw the full moon in the west grow pale and
      disappear in the morning light,
When I wander'd alone over the beach, and undressing
      bathed, laughing with the cool waters, and saw the
      sun rise,
And when I thought how my dear friend my lover was
      on his way coming, O then I was happy,
O then each breath tasted sweeter, and all that day my
      food nourish'd me more, and the beautiful day
      pass'd well,
And the next came with equal joy, and with the next at
      evening came my friend,
And that night while all was still I heard the waters roll
      slowly continually up the shores,
I heard the hissing rustle of the liquid and sands as
      directed to me whispering to congratulate me,
For the one I love most lay sleeping by me under the
      same cover in the cool night,

In the stillness in the autumn moonbeams his face was
    inclined toward me,
And his arm lay lightly around my breast—and that
    night
I was happy.

Morning

Sonnet XXXIII

William Shakespeare

Full many a glorious morning have I seen
Flatter the mountain tops with sovereign eye,
Kissing with golden face the meadows green,
Gilding pale streams with heavenly alchemy;
Anon permit the basest clouds to ride
With ugly rack on his celestial face,
And from the forlorn world his visage hide,
Stealing unseen to west with this disgrace:
Even so my sun one early morn did shine,
With all-triumphant splendour on my brow;
But out, alack, he was but one hour mine,
The region cloud hath mask'd him from me now.
Yet him for this my love no whit disdaineth;
Suns of the world may stain when heaven's sun
staineth.

Composed Upon Westminster Bridge

William Wordsworth

Earth has not anything to show more fair:
Dull would he be of soul who could pass by
A sight so touching in its majesty:
This City now doth, like a garment, wear
The beauty of the morning; silent, bare,
Ships, towers, domes, theatres, and temples lie
Open unto the fields, and to the sky;
All bright and glittering in the smokeless air.
Never did sun more beautifully steep
In his first splendour, valley, rock, or hill;
Ne'er saw I, never felt, a calm so deep!
The river glideth at his own sweet will:
Dear God! the very houses seem asleep;
And all that mighty heart is lying still!

Morning

Paul Laurence Dunbar

The mist has left the greening plain,
The dew-drops shine like fairy rain,
The coquette rose awakes again
    Her lovely self adorning.
The Wind is hiding in the trees,
A sighing, soothing, laughing tease,
Until the rose says "Kiss me, please,"
    'Tis morning, 'tis morning.

With staff in hand and careless-free,
The wanderer fares right jauntily,
For towns and houses are, thinks he,
    For scorning, for scorning.
My soul is swift upon the wing,
And in its deeps a song I bring;
Come, Love, and we together sing,
    "'Tis morning, 'tis morning."

The sun just touched the morning

Emily Dickinson

The sun just touched the morning;
The morning, happy thing,
Supposed that he had come to dwell,
And life would all be spring.

She felt herself supremer,—
A raised, ethereal thing;
Henceforth for her what holiday!
Meanwhile, her wheeling king

Trailed slow along the orchards
His haughty, spangled hems,
Leaving a new necessity,—
The want of diadems!

The morning fluttered, staggered,
Felt feebly for her crown,—
Her unanointed forehead
Henceforth her only one.

The Inward Morning

Henry David Thoreau

Packed in my mind lie all the clothes
    Which outward nature wears,
And in its fashion's hourly change
    It all things else repairs.

In vain I look for change abroad,
    And can no difference find,
Till some new ray of peace uncalled
    Illumes my inmost mind.

What is it gilds the trees and clouds,
    And paints the heavens so gay,
But yonder fast-abiding light
    With its unchanging ray?

Lo, when the sun streams through the wood,
    Upon a winter's morn,
Where'er his silent beams intrude,
    The murky night is gone.

How could the patient pine have known
    The morning breeze would come,
Or humble flowers anticipate
    The insect's noonday hum,—

Till the new light with morning cheer
　　From far streamed through the aisles,
And nimbly told the forest trees
　　For many stretching miles?

I've heard within my inmost soul
　　Such cheerful morning news,
In the horizon of my mind
　　Have seen such orient hues,

As in the twilight of the dawn,
　　When the first birds awake,
Are heard within some silent wood,
　　Where they the small twigs break,

Or in the eastern skies are seen,
　　Before the sun appears,
The harbingers of summer heats
　　Which from afar he bears.

Song on May Morning

John Milton

Now the bright Morning-star, day's harbinger,
Comes dancing from the east, and leads with her
The flowery May, who from her green lap throws
The yellow cowslip and the pale primrose.
    Hail, bounteous May, that dost inspire
    Mirth, and youth, and warm desire;
    Woods and groves are of thy dressing,
    Hill and dale doth boast they blessing.
Thus we salute thee with our early song,
And welcome thee, and wish thee long.

Mattens, or Morning Prayer

Robert Herrick

When with the Virgin morning thou do'st rise,
Crossing thy self; come thus to sacrifice:
First wash thy heart in innocence, then bring
Pure hands, pure habits, pure, pure every thing.
Next to the Altar humbly kneele, and thence
Give up thy soul in clouds of frankincence.
Thy golden censers fill'd with odours sweet,
Shall make thy actions with their ends to meet.

The Sun-Rising

❦

John Donne

Busy old fool, unruly sun,
    Why dost thou thus,
Through windows, and through curtains call on us?
Must to thy motions lovers' seasons run?
    Saucy pedantic wretch, go chide
    Late school-boys, and sour 'prentices,
  Go tell court-huntsmen, that the King will ride,
  Call country ants to harvest offices;
Love, all alike, no season knows nor clime,
Nor hours, days, months, which are the rags of time.

    Thy beams, so reverend and strong
    Dost thou not think?
I could eclipse and cloud them with a wink,
But that I would not lose her sight so long?
    If her eyes have not blinded thine,
    Look, and to-morrow late tell me
  Whether both the Indias of spice and mine
  Be where thou leftst them, or lie here with me;
Ask for those kings, whom thou saw'st yesterday,
And thou shalt hear all here in one bed lay.

    She's all states, and all princes, I,
    Nothing else is.
Princes do but play us; compared to this,
All honor's mimic, all wealth alchemy;

Thou sun art half as happy as we,
    In that the world's contracted thus;
  Thine age asks ease, and since thy duties be
  To warm the world, that's done in warming us.
Shine here to us, and thou art everywhere;
This bed thy center is, these walls, thy sphere.

Morning

Sara Teasdale

I went out on an April morning
    All alone, for my heart was high,
I was a child of the shining meadow,
    I was a sister of the sky.

There in the windy flood of morning
    Longing lifted its weight from me,
Lost as a sob in the midst of cheering,
    Swept as a sea-bird out to sea.

Morning on the Beach

Georgia Wood Pangborn

Some brighter thing than sunlight touched the sea
And out of dawn arose a wind of joy:
They woke and chirped—my girl, and then my boy—
Like birds that have not learned what fears there be.
"And now," I thought, "there dawns a day to me:
One day, at least, defies moon-prophecies;
One day shall call the old world sorrows lies,
So let us now be happy utterly."

Then we had playmates in the grains of sand—
I heard them, many-laughing, by the water;
The sweet air thrilled to speech without a tongue.
Then met my boy and led him by the hand
To venturous depths, they showed my little daughter
How children built on sand when time was young.

Marriage Morning

Alfred, Lord Tennyson

Light, so low upon earth,
　　You send a flash to the sun.
Here is the golden close of love,
　　All my wooing is done.
Oh, all the woods and the meadows,
　　Woods, where we hid from the wet,
Stiles where we stayed to be kind,
　　Meadows in which we met!

Light, so low in the vale
　　You flash and lighten afar,
For this is the golden morning of love,
　　And you are his morning star.
Flash, I am coming, I come,
　　By meadow and stile and wood,
Oh, lighten into my eyes and my heart,
　　Into my heart and my blood!

Heart, are you great enough
　　For a love that never tires?
O heart, are you great enough for love?
　　I have heard of thorns and briers.
Over the thorns and briers,
　　Over the meadows and stiles,
Over the world to the end of it
　　Flash of a million miles.

Departed Days

Oliver Wendell Holmes

Yes, dear departed, cherished days,
　　Could Memory's hand restore
Your morning light, your evening rays,
　　From Time's gray urn once more,
Then might this restless heart be still,
　　This straining eye might close,
And Hope her fainting pinions fold,
　　While the fair phantoms rose.

But, like a child in ocean's arms,
　　We strive against the stream,
Each moment farther from the shore
　　Where life's young fountains gleam;
Each moment fainter wave the fields,
　　And wider rolls the sea;
The mist grows dark,—the sun goes down,—
　　Day breaks,—and where are we?

The Day Ahead

A Dream

Edgar Allan Poe

In visions of the dark night
    I have dreamed of joy departed—
But a waking dream of life and light
    Hath left me broken-hearted.

Ah! what is not a dream by day
    To him whose eyes are cast
On things around him with a ray
    Turned back upon the past?

That holy dream—that holy dream,
    While all the world were chiding,
Hath cheered me as a lovely beam
    A lonely spirit guiding.

What though that light, thro' storm and night,
    So trembled from afar—
What could there be more purely bright
    In Truths day-star?

Mutation

William Cullen Bryant

They talk of short-lived pleasure—be it so—
   Pain dies as quickly: stern, hard-featured pain
Expires, and lets her weary prisoner go.
   The fiercest agonies have shortest reign;
   And after dreams of horror, comes again
The welcome morning with its rays of peace.
   Oblivion, softly wiping out the stain,
Makes the strong secret pangs of shame to cease:
Remorse is virtue's root; its fair increase
   Are fruits of innocence and blessedness:
Thus joy, o'erborne and bound, doth still release
   His young limbs from the chains that round him press.
Weep not that the world changes—did it keep
A stable, changeless state, 'twere cause indeed to weep.

Parting at Morning

Robert Browning

Round the cape of a sudden came the sea,
And the sun looked over the mountain's rim:
And straight was a path of gold for him,
And the need of a world of men for me.

Morning Prayer

Ella Wheeler Wilcox

Let me to-day do something that shall take
    A little sadness from the world's vast store,
And may I be so favoured as to make
    Of joy's too scanty sum a little more.
Let me not hurt, by any selfish deed
    Or thoughtless word, the heart of foe or friend;
Nor would I pass, unseeing, worthy need,
    Or sin by silence when I should defend.
However meagre be my worldly wealth,
    Let me give something that shall aid my kind—
A word of courage, or a thought of health,
    Dropped as I pass for troubled hearts to find.
Let me to-night look back across the span
    'Twixt dawn and dark, and to my conscience say—
Because of some good act to beast or man—
    "The world is better that I lived to-day."

God's Grandeur

Gerard Manley Hopkins

The world is charged with the grandeur of God.
    It will flame out, like shining from shook foil;
    It gathers to a greatness, like the ooze of oil
Crushed. Why do men then now not reck his rod?
Generations have trod, have trod, have trod;
      And all is seared with trade; bleared, smeared with
        toil;
      And wears man's smudge and shares man's smell:
        the soil
Is bare now, nor can foot feel, being shod.

And for all this, nature is never spent;
    There lives the dearest freshness deep down things;
And though the last lights off the black West went
    Oh, morning, at the brown brink eastward,
        springs—
Because the Holy Ghost over the bent
    World broods with warm breast and with ah!
        bright wings.

On a Fine Morning

Thomas Hardy

I

Whence comes Solace?—Not from seeing
What is doing, suffering, being,
Not from noting Life's conditions,
Nor from heeding Time's monitions;
    But in cleaving to the Dream,
    And in gazing at the gleam
    Whereby gray things golden seem.

II

Thus do I this heyday, holding
Shadows but as lights unfolding,
As no specious show this moment
With its iris-hued embowment;
    But as nothing other than
    Part of a benignant plan;
    Proof that earth was made for man.

Home

~❦~

Edward Thomas

Fair was the morning, fair our tempers, and
We had seen nothing fairer than that land,
Though strange, and the untrodden snow that made
Wild of the tame, casting out all that was
Not wild and rustic and old; and we were glad.

Fair, too, was afternoon, and first to pass
Were we that league of snow, next the north wind.

There was nothing to return for, except need,
And yet we sang nor ever stopped for speed,
As we did often with the start behind.
Faster still strode we when we came in sight
Of the cold roofs where we must spend the night.
Happy we had not been there, nor could be.
Though we had tasted sleep and food and fellowship
Together long.

        "How quick" to someone's lip
The words came, "will the beaten horse run home."

The word "home" raised a smile in us all three,
And one repeated it, smiling just so
That all knew what he meant and none would say.
Between three counties far apart that lay

We were divided and looked strangely each
At the other, and we knew we were not friends
But fellows in a union that ends
With the necessity for it, as it ought.

Never a word was spoken, not a thought
Was thought, of what the look meant with the word
"Home" as we walked and watched the sunset blurred.
And then to me the word, only the word,
"Homesick," as it were playfully occurred:
No more.

    If I should ever more admit
Than the mere word I could not endure it
For a day longer: this captivity
Must somehow come to an end, else I should be
Another man, as often now I seem,
Or this life be only an evil dream.

Futility

Wilfred Owen

Move him into the sun—
Gently its touch awoke him once,
At home, whispering of fields unsown.
Always it woke him, even in France,
Until this morning and this snow.
If anything might rouse him now
The kind old sun will know.

Think how it wakes the seeds—
Woke, once, the clays of a cold star.
Are limbs so dear-achieved, are sides
Full-nerved,—still warm,—too hard to stir?
Was it for this the clay grew tall?
—O what made fatuous sunbeams toil
To break earth's sleep at all?

Days

Ralph Waldo Emerson

Daughters of Time, the hypocritic Days,
Muffled and dumb like barefoot dervishes,
And marching single in an endless file,
Bring diadems and fagots in their hands.
To each they offer gifts after his will,
Bread, kingdoms, stars, or sky that holds them all.
I, in my pleached garden, watched the pomp,
Forgot my morning wishes, hastily
Took a few herbs and apples, and the Day
Turned and departed silent. I, too late,
Under her solemn fillet saw the scorn.

Breakfast

❧

Mary Lamb

A dinner party, coffee, tea,
Sandwich, or supper, all may be
In their way pleasant. But to me
Not one of these deserves the praise
That welcomer of new-born days,
A *breakfast*, merits; ever giving
Cheerful notice we are living
Another day refreshed by sleep,
When its festival we keep.
Now although I would not slight
Those kindly words we use "Good night,"
Yet parting words are words of sorrow,
And may not vie with sweet "Good Morrow,"
With which again our friends we greet,
When in the breakfast-room we meet,
At the social table round,
Listening to the lively sound
Of those notes which never tire,
Of urn, or kettle on the fire.
Sleepy Robert never hears
Or urn, or kettle; he appears
When all have finished, one by one
Dropping off, and breakfast done.
Yet has he too his own pleasure,
His breakfast hour's his hour of leisure;

And, left alone, he reads or muses,
Or else in idle mood he uses
To sit and watch the vent'rous fly,
Where the sugar's piled high,
Clambering o'er the lumps so white,
Rocky cliffs of sweet delight.

Early to Bed

Mary Mapes Dodge

Early to bed and early to rise:
If *that* would make me wealthy and wise
I'd rise at daybreak, cold or hot,
And go back to bed at once. Why not?

Signature Select Classics

Elegantly Designed Booklets of Poetry and Prose

This book is part of Sterling Publishing's Signature Select Classics chapbook series. Each booklet features distinguished poetry and prose by the world's greatest poets and writers in an elegantly designed and printed chapbook binding. These books are essential reading for lovers of classic literature and collectible editions in their own right. They make perfect keepsakes to own and to share with others.